JUST THE GREATEST

CARL NELSON

Carl Nelson

To Angela

InterVarsity Press
Downers Grove, Illinois 60515

Second printing, February 1974

InterVarsity Press is the book
publishing division of Inter-Varsity
Christian Fellowship, a student
movement active on campus at
hundreds of universities, colleges
and schools of nursing. For
information about this dynamic
association, write IVCF, 233 Langdon,
Madison, WI 53703. If you're a
student, four chances out of five
you'll find a local IVCF chapter on
your campus.

The Scripture passages designated
"Phillips" are reprinted with
permission of The Macmillan
Company from The New Testament
in Modern English by J. B. Phillips.
© J. B. Phillips 1958

The Scripture passages designated
"RSV" are from the Revised Standard
Version of the Bible, copyrighted
1946 and 1952 by the Division of
Christian Education of the National
Council of the Churches of Christ in
the U.S.A. and used by permission.

ISBN 0-87784-543-3
Library of Congress Catalog
Card Number: 72-184953

Printed in the United
States of America

contents

1
No Kidding

"You're the most beautiful girl," he said. And she, assuming he meant in the whole world, glowed in the wonder of what she had just heard and stopped listening. But he was still talking. "You're the most beautiful girl in this school," he continued. That still would have been quite a compliment, especially since the school was large—1,829 kids, not counting yesterday's dropouts—but he hadn't finished yet. "You're the most beautiful, junior, red-haired girl named Judy on this campus," he concluded. Actually if she had kept listening, she would have realized that he had said that in a particular limited group of two she was the more beautiful.

This reminds me of one of my professors in graduate school who was an authority on religious books. Because of his reputation he was often asked to review and recommend them. He became adept at saying glowing things about all good books.

As a student in his class I remember the first time he recommended a book. He began, "This is the greatest book. . . ." I hurried to write it down. After all, he was an authority. I have since forgotten the book he recommended, but his words went something like this: "This is the greatest book written by an Englishman in the past decade on the subject of evolution from a theistic point of view." When I reread what he had said, it dawned on me that it was altogether possible that there was only one book written by an Englishman in the past decade on the subject of evolution from a theistic point of view.

Superlatives are used so often in our day that they hardly faze us. Television ads, for example, have portrayed the greatest detergent, the greatest deodorant, the greatest automobile and so on until the greatest is not much different from the commonplace.

For years *Esquire, Sports Illustrated, Time,* and the Butte Community High School Year Book (*The Wildcat*) have designated the Man of the Year, the Athlete of the Decade, the Ten Best Dressed Women, Miss America, the Man Most Likely to Succeed and Mother of the Year.

All of this makes it difficult to catch the impact of this next sentence. You see, I want to let you in on the greatest event in the history of the world.

Now, right away our regulated minds want to limit that statement. Don't you mean the greatest event in the last ten years or last hundred years? Or perhaps you intended to say the greatest event in North America or Europe or maybe even in Denver, Colorado, or London, England. Or at least you were certainly limiting yourself to the greatest religious or athletic or political event.

No, I meant what I said. I want to talk about the greatest event in the history of the world—no limiting clauses of time or place or type or anything else. The greatest.

2
What on Earth Could It Be?

"What is the greatest event in the history of the world?" If someone asked you, what would you say?

Now it is altogether possible that you have never given this question any serious thought at all. That would not be surprising.

Some time ago I read about a group of intelligent, educated men who got together to discuss this very question. After a great deal of discussion, they came to the conclusion that the greatest single event in the history of the world was the discovery of the wheel.

When I first read this, I thought it was ridiculous. Then, the more I thought about it, the more I realized what a significant event the discovery of the wheel actually was.

Think about it for a while. How different would your life be if it were not for the wheel? Consider that set of wheels called the automobile. It takes us to football games and rock festivals, to school and to drive-ins, to see grandmother and Judy, and to visit Florida and California. Nearly everything we own —the clothes we wear, the food we eat, the furniture we use, the books and newspapers we read—could not even be manufactured without wheels, let alone get to us.

There's no doubt about it, the invention of the wheel was a very important event in the history of the world. But as great as it was, I don't think it was the greatest—not for a moment.

I have been told that another group of men came to a different conclusion about the greatest event in history. The discovery of America, they said. Whoever discovered America—the Italians, the Norwegians, the Hebrews, the Spaniards, the Africans—it was indeed a very important event.

Now I live in America and I'm grateful to the explorers who discovered it. Land is hard to come by and men need all the space they can get. Who knows, many of the important things that have taken place on this continent might never have happened, if it had not been for that original discovery. The discovery of America was important, but certainly not the greatest thing that ever happened.

In our day men have landed on the moon. President Nixon and others have termed this event the greatest since creation. Is it? Some say it was a waste of money. Only time will tell how important this feat is. There is no doubt about it, landing men on the moon is a fantastic achievement. It is possible also that it will open immensely valuable doors to the human race. But as important as this event may prove to be, I still don't think that it's the most important event in history.

I am sure that many other significant events have been chosen as the greatest. Here's the one I'm convinced is really the greatest.

The greatest event that ever took place in the history of the world is the crucifixion of Jesus Christ outside Jerusalem nearly 2,000 years ago.

At the outset, I realize that there are some seeming weaknesses to this choice. We usually think of greatness as something that happens in a man's life, not in his death. Still, all of us can remember or imagine situations in which the greatest thing that an individual might do would be to die. Giving one's life to save other lives may overshadow anything else in a person's life. Heroic death we understand and honor.

But the death of Jesus Christ was not so heroic. He was executed as a common criminal. How can the execution of a man even be considered significant, let alone the greatest **13** thing that ever happened?

Besides that, there was nothing unique about a crucifixion. It was the standard Roman method of executing criminals who were not Roman citizens. Two other men were crucified with Jesus. How many others were crucified that same year outside the city of Jerusalem? Were there five, ten, or perhaps more? Over the years that the Romans were in charge in Jerusalem, how many men were crucified at that place called Calvary? And consider all the cities and towns that were a part of the conquered Roman empire. How many people were crucified during these years? Certainly hundreds, perhaps thousands, it is hard to say. Whatever the number, certainly a crucifixion was not unique. Ordinarily when a man was crucified few people watched—the assigned soldiers, a weeping mother, perhaps a friend or compatriot. A crucifixion was considered neither important nor unique.

But with all these seeming negative associations, I am still convinced that the greatest event that ever took place was the crucifixion of Jesus Christ outside the city of Jerusalem. To hold this idea, I had better have some good reasons, and I believe I do. You may not agree with me, and that is your privilege, but take a look and decide for yourself.

3
Who Was He?

When two Little League baseball teams play, you can be almost sure that all of the spectators are related to the players. To mom and dad, Junior's game is very important, but to the rest of the world it's not.

On the other hand, when fall rolls around and it's time for the World Series, the winners of the American League and the National League pennants can pack out any stadium in our country. And while thousands are watching in person, millions more observe this classic on television. Nearly every baseball fan takes a special interest in the World Series. In fact, quite a few people who are not even interested in baseball somehow become interested in the World Series.

It's obvious that the importance of a base-ball game depends a great deal on who is playing.

If you and some of your friends decided to organize a musical group and then to tour the country giving concerts, you would probably have a difficult time getting large crowds or possibly even small crowds. But from time to time there have been groups like the Beatles and the Stones who—while they held to-gether—consistently packed out the houses. As soon as they are booked, people rush to buy tickets. Which all goes to prove that the importance of any concert depends a great deal on who is performing.

During election year when the candidates for the highest office are going from city to city making speeches, they are met by vast crowds. This same response would be nearly impossible to anyone else.

No doubt—the importance of any event de-pends on who is involved. And my first reason for believing that the greatest event in the his-tory of the world is the crucifixion of Jesus Christ is who it was who died there that day. Who was he? Who was this person known as Jesus Christ?

There is an incident in the life of Jesus that is particularly interesting to me.[1] Perhaps it is because I was in the Navy for three years and on an aircraft carrier in the South Pacific for nearly a year. During this time we got into a couple of pretty bad storms, and I hate to admit it, but I was scared.

This incident in Jesus' life took place on the Sea of Galilee. He had been talking to a crowd on the beach. And because the crowd was so large, he had gotten into one of the boats and was speaking to the people from there. That evening after he had finished talking to the people, he told his disciples that he wanted to go to the other side of the lake.

And so they began their journey across the Sea of Galilee. On their way, a storm came up. I have read that on this sea a severe storm can come up rather quickly. Some of the disciples in the boat with Jesus that day were fishermen; they had been fishermen all their lives and their fathers before them had been fishermen. They had spent many hours on the Sea of Galilee and you can be sure they had been there during many storms.

When the storm first came up, they began almost automatically to do what sailors and fishermen do during a storm. Then, as the storm progressed, I can imagine Peter yelling to Andrew above the noise of the wind: "Hey, Andrew, some storm." And then if you and I could have been there that day, I think we would have seen a tenseness begin in Peter's face as he began to realize that this was one of the worst storms he had ever been in on the Sea of Galilee. And then we would see this tenseness become actual fear as Peter realized that he had done all he could do and it was not enough and that before long the ship would sink and they would all be lost.

At this point they remembered Jesus. He was relaxed and asleep and it seemed to frustrate them that he could be so cool at a time like this. Irritated, they woke him and demanded: "Don't you care if we perish?" I don't know whether they expected him to do anything or not. But they certainly weren't prepared for what he did do. For he stood up and yelled at the wind and said to the sea: "Peace, be still." And the wind ceased and there was a great calm.

If someone had stood up on the flight deck of the *U.S.S. Siboney* during a storm in the Pacific and rebuked the wind and said to the sea, "Shut up!" and it became still, I, along with all the other sailors aboard, would have been filled with utter awe and probably fear and wondered who on earth this person could be who could do such a thing.

And that is exactly the reaction that the disciples had on the Sea of Galilee, for it says that they were filled with awe and said to one another: "Who, then, is this that even the wind and the sea obey him?" The men who asked this question were men who were already convinced that Jesus was a great person, that he indeed was someone special for they had left their jobs to follow him. But this event forced them to ask the question more deeply: "Who, then, is this that even the wind and the sea obey him?"

You can be sure that in the next hours and days and months they watched more closely what he did and listened more closely to what he said. They saw him give eyes to the blind, ears to the deaf, legs to the lame, health to the diseased, wholeness to the deranged and life to the dead.

They heard the ring of truth and authority in his words. When some of Jesus' fringe followers left him, and he asked the disciples if they, too, would leave, they answered, "To whom should we go? You have the words of eternal life."[2]

And they observed the character of his life. They were with him day in and day out for nearly three solid years. They saw him in all kinds of trying circumstances and situations, and it was their studied conclusion that he never did one single, solitary thing wrong. No one says that about you or me, but they said it about Jesus.

And when these eye witnesses had had a full opportunity to observe him and to think about what they saw, they concluded that Jesus Christ was God.

They were convinced that the eternal son of God—who, with his Father, created all that is—had taken on human form and lived with them. John writes in the first chapter of his portrait of Christ that this One, this Word, who was God, who was with God in the beginning, by whom all things were created, became a man and lived with us and we knew him as Jesus Christ.[3]

But as you hear these stupendous conclusions, your inclination may be to say that you haven't had the chance to see Jesus and so you aren't all that impressed. Or you may be inclined to say, "How do I know that these things the Bible talks about ever really happened?"

Let me ask you a question, "What's the date today?" Whatever the day is, if you think about it a while, you'll realize that the date is so many years since Jesus Christ was born. When we study history, we use terms B.C. and A.D. since all time is dated by Jesus Christ. Perhaps just as the disciples on the Sea of Galilee asked themselves, "Who, then, is this that even the wind and the sea obey him?" we too should ask ourselves, "Who, then, is this that we should calculate all history by him?"

And how come we in a land thousands of miles away from his birthplace, nearly 2,000 years later, in an entirely different culture, celebrate his birthday, Christmas, as the biggest holiday of the year?

And how can we explain all the churches that dot our land and our world? In a sense each steeple is a monument to Jesus, indicating he was someone special. Most of us could not even begin to name the presidents of the United States—only a few of them are known to all. Perhaps only Washington, Lincoln and Jefferson have monuments of any significance built to them. But Jesus Christ has monuments built to him all over the world.

He did not rule a country, he did not lead an army, he did not travel extensively or write a book. He did not do any of the things men usually must do to be remembered. And yet by the very impact of his life, by his influence on the world around him, he comes to us as the one by whom we date all time. Who, then, is he?

I have considered the evidence and have come to the same conclusion as his disciples: God was here—the eternal son of God took on flesh and lived on this earth.

But every once in a while you hear someone say that Jesus himself did not claim to be God. Now, it is true that he did not go around carrying a sign saying, "I am God." But the evidence of the earliest documents points to the fact that Jesus considered himself to be God.

For example, speaking of his Father in heaven, he flatly said, "I and the Father are one."[4] At another place in a discussion about himself and Abraham, he said, "Before Abraham was, I am."[5] He was claiming eternity and also using a term, "I Am," which was reserved in the Old Testament for God. When a man bowed before Jesus one day and worshipped him, Jesus did not discourage him but accepted that worship.[6] Years later when men bowed before the great apostle Paul to worship him, he quickly told them to get up since he was a man just like they were.[7]

Again, when Jesus stood on trial and the judge asked him if he was the Christ, he said, "I am, and you will see the Son of Man sitting at the right hand of power and coming with the clouds of heaven."[8] Traditionally, the phrase, "Son of Man" was used only of a divine person. So when they heard Jesus attach this phrase to himself, they ripped their clothes, claiming that Jesus was being blasphemous, that here was a man actually claiming to be God. Jesus did not contradict them or say that they had misunderstood him. He had said what he had meant to say, and they had understood.

Because Jesus Christ claimed to be God, we are forced to make one of three conclusions: He was either a liar (he knew he wasn't God but he said he was), or he was insane (he actually thought he was God but wasn't), or he was actually who he claimed to be (he was God).

If someone starts walking around the halls of your high school with his hand in his shirt claiming to be Napoleon, you have to come to one of these three conclusions. First, he really is Napoleon. This, of course, is highly improbable. Second, he is lying. This is much more probable, for perhaps he's just trying to be funny. But if day after day this boy goes around claiming to be Napoleon, it would not be long before we would come to the conclusion that something had gone wrong upstairs, and soon it would be necessary for some nice men in little white suits to come and take him to a place where he could enjoy being with other great men such as Alexander the Great and Julius Caesar.

Some people want to say that Jesus was just a good man, a good man that said great things, but not a God. Such a view is not possible. Jesus was either God, or a fake or a nut. And the facts of his life and his influence on history do not support the last two. The facts of the life of Jesus show that he was a man of integrity and honesty and decency, and not a liar. They also show that he was a man of stability and dependability and not a man who was mentally deranged. If anyone accepts the opinion that Jesus was a fraud or insane, they are also faced with accepting that we date all time by a man who was either one of the greatest frauds or one of the most confused men who ever lived.

But the disciples who had the best opportunity to observe his life concluded that he was, in fact, who he claimed to be—God in human form. And my first reason for believing that the crucifixion of Jesus Christ outside Jerusalem nearly 2,000 years ago is the greatest event that ever happened in the history of the world is the nature of the person who died there—God in human form, the eternal incarnate son of God.

4
Time Out for a Wedding

So much has changed in the last fifty years—in fact, even in the last few years—that one wonders whether anything is permanent. But even a casual observation shows that some things stay pretty much the same. Today a boy and girl meet and fall in love. That happened yesterday, the day before, 200 years ago, and even 2,000 years before that.

When Jesus was on earth, there were a boy and girl who lived in the city of Cana. They met, fell in love and got married. We do not know any of the details of the romance. Perhaps it began one day as he was walking down the halls of South Cana High and noticed how good she looked and decided that he had better get to know her better. Actually it probably didn't happen that way since girls usually did not go to school in those days. Possibly these two had known each other since they were little kids and he was simply marrying his childhood sweetheart.

Of course, we know in those days parents often got into the act and set up marriages themselves. Even so, it is hard for me to imagine that the boy and girl had nothing to say about it. Perhaps one night this boy asked for the opportunity to speak to his father and told him how he felt about this particular girl and wondered if his dad would speak to her parents and see if a marriage could be arranged. However it happened, the day came when they were to be married.

Among the guests invited to the wedding feast was Jesus.[1] I suppose some people would assume that he would be too busy giving sermons and having religious discussions to come to a wedding. But Jesus Christ was interested in people and in the things that were important to them, so he accepted the invitation and came to the wedding.

This incident in Jesus' life has always interested me, but it took on an added dimension recently when I found out that Cana was a poverty area. The two kids getting married that day had probably never known what it was to have enough of anything, and it was probably a strain on the family finances to have a wedding feast. But this was a big occasion, and they went all out to make it the finest they could, and like all young couples —especially the bride—they wanted to have everything just right on this important day of their lives.

Before the feast was over, it was apparent to those serving that they soon would run out of wine. And for a moment, it looked like it was going to be the same old story—never having enough of anything—and even this happy day would have to carry that blot. One of the first people who knew they were running out of wine was the mother of Jesus. She called for some servants and told them to do whatever her son Jesus told them to do.

After a brief hesitation, he told them to fill six very large jars with water, and when they had done this, he told them to draw some out and take it to the master of ceremonies. You can imagine how these servants felt. They well knew that the water supply was not good to drink. To make matters worse, it would be a sorry substitute for wine at a wedding feast. I'm sure that the servants could imagine losing their jobs and even their union cards, but they did what Jesus said.

Perhaps they did it because of the quality of his life and the confidence he instilled in them. Or perhaps as they looked at the water, they began to see what was already happening. At any rate, when the master of ceremonies tasted the water which by Jesus' power had now become wine, he said, "Everybody I know puts his good wine on first and then when men have had plenty to drink he brings out the poor stuff, but you have kept back your good wine until now."

This was the first time that Jesus had used his extraordinary power. His disciples saw it and believed. It was one of those many incidents in his life that made them come to their thoughtful conclusion—this man Jesus was God in human form.[2] Here was the Creator at work before their very eyes. Without the necessary ingredients of grapes and time, he had created wine.

But there is something else exciting about this incident. It not only helps us to know who Jesus Christ was but what he was like. If someone else had the power to make water into wine, he might well have interrupted the wedding ceremony and gotten attention for himself. With every eye focused on him, he could have made quite a display, taking the contaminated water and making it into the best wine people had drunk that day, or perhaps on any day. And then, having displayed this unusual power, he might have announced that he was going into business and from this spectacular moment he could have launched a real going enterprise.

But not so with Jesus Christ. The wedding feast was not upset in any way. The master of ceremonies did not realize where the wine had come from, and I feel that the bride and groom had no idea whatsoever what had

taken place. Probably only the servants, Jesus'
mother and the disciples who were nearby
saw what went on.

It was possibly days, weeks or even
months before the young couple learned what
had taken place. And I feel certain as they
looked back to that day and thought about
what Jesus had done to make it so happy,
they said to one another, "Aren't you glad
that we invited Jesus?" And from this incident we see not only the power and deity of
Jesus Christ but his attractiveness and interest
in people as well. And since that time until
now, thousands of people have found it true
that when they invite Jesus Christ into their
lives, he adds a dimension and a quality that
nothing or no one else can. When Jesus made
the water into wine, he made it into the best
wine. And so from the life of Jesus we find
out not only that God was here, but that
when he was here he was beautiful.

5
The Crime of It All

A few years ago in Lincoln, Nebraska, lived a young man named Charles Starkweather. From all I have read, he was not outstanding. In fact, the opposite was closer to the truth. He had always done poorly in school and finally became a dropout. Once out of school, he had difficulty in finding and keeping a job. He worked for some time collecting garbage. Except for a striking but undeveloped talent for painting, apparently there was only one thing at which he had ever really excelled. He was an excellent marksman with a rifle.

One day Charlie went over to his girl-friend's house and got into an argument with her parents. This was not the first time they had argued, and that day Charlie decided to end it once and for all. He went out to his car, got his rifle and killed his girlfriend's mother, stepfather and her three-year-old stepsister.

In the days that followed, Charles Starkweather struck terror all across Nebraska as he sought to elude police. By the time he was captured some days later in Wyoming, he had killed eleven people. Two were a high school couple who had been kind enough to pick up him and his girlfriend when his car ran out of gas. Charlie killed them both, threw their bodies in a cave and stole their car.

After being captured in Wyoming, he was brought to trial, convicted of first degree murder and sentenced to die in the electric chair.

It just so happened that on the day that Charles Starkweather was executed, I was traveling across Nebraska on my way to Chicago. Driving alone, I turned on the radio to help pass the time. The regular programming was continually interrupted with reports of Starkweather's last day—his last meal, his last visitors and the last attempts to get a pardon for his life.

Also the news reported that hundreds of people had gathered at the state penitentiary at Lincoln where he was to be executed. Thousands of people were listening to the radio for reports leading up to the time the switch would be thrown. It was obvious that this execution had become a big event in the state. My first reaction was that all these people were pretty morbid and that it was unnatural to take such an interest in a man's execution. Nevertheless, my curiosity was aroused.

Now I have already told you that I believe that the greatest event in the history of the world is the execution of Jesus Christ, and I have told you that my first reason for believing that it was the greatest event is who it was who died there—the very quality and importance of the one who died. By no stretch of the imagination can we say that the execution of Charles Starkweather was important because of the quality of Charles Starkweather. That was obviously not the reason.

The more I thought about it, the more obvious it became that the reason Starkweather's execution was important was that his crimes were so heinous. Charles Starkweather did not kill just one or two or three or even five; he killed eleven people. Besides that, most of them he had never seen before. They had never done anything to hurt him. One of his victims was a three-year-old girl. Two had actually sought to help him when he needed it. It is possible that other people would have been murdered if they had not become terrified, locked themselves in their own homes and stayed off the streets.

Now people gathered and people listened— people who had lost a son or a daughter, a mother or a father, a friend or a relative, and others who had perhaps known more terror than they had ever known before when Charles Starkweather came through their neighborhood. Perhaps these people hoped that an awful chapter in their own lives would be finished when Charles Starkweather came to his end. Whatever the case, his execution had become very important, and that was because of the crimes for which he was dying.

So my second reason for believing that the crucifixion of Jesus Christ outside the city of Jerusalem nearly 2,000 years ago was the most important event in the history of the world is the crime for which he died.

What was Jesus' crime? The normal way to answer this question is to go to the record of the trial. But when we do this with Jesus, we find the judge who sentenced him to death saying, "I find nothing criminal about him at all."[1] To add impact to what the judge himself said, the man who betrayed him for thirty pieces of silver later committed suicide, admitting that he had betrayed an innocent man.[2] We have already mentioned what those who were closest to him said about him. They said he had never done anything wrong—not only had he not done anything worthy of execution, he had never done anything wrong at all.[3]

Is this, then, what makes his death important, that a great, good and innocent man dies? No, I think not. Over the history of the world, many innocent men have been executed.

What was it, then? We find the answer in the Apostle Paul's letter to the Roman Christians: "Christ died for our sins."[4] It means that when he died there that day, he was dying for your crimes and my crimes and for the crimes of all the people who had ever lived or who were to live.[5] The Bible uses the word *sin,* but it could just as well use the word *crime.* Perhaps the difference is that we usually refer to breaking the civil law as crime and to breaking God's law as sin.

Before we seek to clarify this further, I think you can begin to see why I believe this is the greatest event in the history of the world. For if Christ died for the crimes of all mankind, then no man can say, "This has nothing to do with me." We were all involved in what happened that day outside of Jerusalem.

But about this time I imagine that some of you, at least, are thinking that you are as good as the next person and that you find it difficult to classify yourself as a criminal or a sinner. You might be inclined to answer that you seek to live by the Golden Rule or by the Ten Commandments or that you put a pretty high priority on trying to be sincere.

Some of you may want to push it back further and say that you do not think there is a God, and that since there is no God there is no law of God for you to keep or break, and therefore no place for guilt or need for somebody to die for your crimes. Without going into the question of whether or not there is a God, let me point out that if there is no God, then for all ethical purposes man is God. You are God and I am God, or mankind in general is God. And let's be honest—you make a lousy god, and I make a lousy god, too. You and I have done some pretty dumb things in our lives. There are some pretty big hurts and unsatisfied questions.

Take a look at the history of the world. Take a look at the miserable job that men have done of running our world. We've made some exciting progress in going to the moon but little or none toward getting along as individuals, families, nations or races. If man is God, we're doomed.

To my way of thinking, the evidence for the existence of God is overwhelming, and the vast majority of people in our country would also say that they believe there is a God. Of course, some of these people have not taken much time or trouble to learn much about this God that they believe exists.

The Bible says that God created everything that is, and not only did he create natural laws by which this universe was to work, but he also gave some moral laws that he expected his created men to live by. The best-known statement of God's laws are the laws that we usually refer to as the Ten Commandments.[6]

Let's look at some of the Ten Commandments to test ourselves, to check ourselves out, as it were, to see whether we have kept or broken God's laws. You do not have to tell me how you do on this test; you do not have to tell anybody else how you do on this test. And fortunately I don't have to tell you. But it would be a very good idea for each of us to find out just where he stands before God.

One of the commandments says, "You shall not steal." This commandment does not mean merely "Do not be a professional thief." It could be stated, "Don't take anything that doesn't belong to you." This would include not taking answers from someone else's paper on a test. In other words, don't cheat. I am not sure how it is at your school, but I get the feeling that there is an awful lot of cheating going on. In the past several years at the Air Force Academy there have been two major cheating scandals. And this is a school that has the opportunity to choose from the cream of the crop of the nation's high school students. The attitude seems to be: "It's okay if you can get by with it." But don't forget that God said, "Don't take anything that doesn't belong to you."

This could even include taking pay from an employer when you know good and well that you have not put in your time in any meaningful way. From the way people talk, there are many people who are employed who are not doing any more than they have to. Do not take anything that does not belong to you.

A druggist in Knoxville, Tennessee, who was going out of business told me the reason he had to quit was not merely that the competition was stiff but that students from a nearby high school took so many items without paying that it was impossible for him to make a basic profit. A high school boy confessed to me once that at the convention of an outstanding high school club some of the boys spent the afternoon free time seeing how much they could steal in a certain period of time from the nearby department stores.

Well, how are you doing on this test so far? Don't tell me, but be sure to be honest with yourself.

Another commandment says, "You shall not bear false witness against your neighbor." In other words, don't say something about someone else that is not true. It seems to me that people of all ages spend a lot of time sitting around talking about other people. If I understand things correctly, truth does not seem to be the important factor. Things are said that really are untrue or only half true. Perhaps behind this is people's own desire to be on top. They think that cutting someone else down might have the result of making themselves look better. At any rate, a lot of people are hurt—some seriously—because others have been willing to pass on lies about them. God says, "Don't say something about someone else that is not true." How is your record on this one?

Here is another one: "Honor your father and mother." That is, show proper respect to your parents. At another place the Bible says to obey your parents.[7] Now, I'm well aware that parents are not always right. In fact, they are capable of some pretty wretched things. But God was well aware of this when he gave the commandment and he gave it anyway.

I've been downright embarrassed at times when I have been with some high school students and their parents. It was obvious that they were not showing proper respect. I could not help but wonder that if they acted this way toward their parents when someone else was around how they acted when they were alone with their family. Does the way you act toward your parents and the way you talk about your parents with your own high school friends honor them? God said, "Honor your father and your mother."

Another commandment states, "You shall not commit adultery." I am confident that this commandment includes more than what might be legally included in the word *adultery*. I believe this because of the way God speaks about sex in other places in the Bible. For example, in the letter to the Romans, Paul writes, "Let us live cleanly as in the daylight, not in the 'delights' of getting drunk or playing with sex. . . ."[8] A rather loose but legitimate way to state this commandment would be, "Don't mess around with sex."

God created sex and called it good, and there is no doubt that sex is significant and important. But God set some moral limits to protect this beautiful thing he had created. So he says to people, "Don't mess around with it."

You and I live in a day that entertains loose ideas in regard to sex. The Playboy philosophy is in vogue and there are all sorts of pressures on us to make us conform. There is a lot of talk in our day about sex and lots of surveys on sexual behavior. I'm sure that some of these articles are written more to sell magazines than to tell facts. Some of them overstate for effect. But you have a pretty good idea of what goes on at your school. The commandment says, "You shall not commit adultery." Don't play with something sacred.

We could consider all the commandments, but take a look at just one more, the very first one. It says, "You shall have no other gods before me." Perhaps our first reaction is that we are okay on this one. We don't have any gods made of wood or metal around the house that we bow down and worship, and there is no animal or part of the universe that we have made sacred. But when it comes right down to it, a god is that person or thing that we consider to be supreme. It is the number one thing in our lives.

How about you? What is your god? Is it football? Or pot? Or popularity? Or peace? Or a certain person? Or a certain group of people? Or is it money and what money can buy? The thing is this—what controls your life?

From years of observation, it doesn't seem to me that there are very many people whose guiding principle of life is what God wants them to do. For most people the crowd around them influences them much more than God does. Not only is God not number one, he is way down on the list, or maybe he does not even appear there. You'll have to answer for yourself how you have done on this most important commandment.

I don't want you to tell me how you did on this test, but I'll admit that I believe I know how you came out if you were honest with yourself. But just in case you slipped up, let me point out that God who knows everything about you has already scored your exam. Again the letter to the Romans states,

There is none righteous, no, not one.
There is none that understandeth,
There is none that seeketh after God;
They have all turned aside; they are
together become as unprofitable;
There is none that doeth good, no not so
much as one: . . .
There is no fear of God before their
eyes. . . . Indeed it is the straightedge of
the Law that shows us how crooked we
are. . . . For there is no distinction to be
made anywhere: every one has sinned;
every one falls short of the beauty of
God's plan.[9]

God, knowing us as we are, has concluded that each one of us has broken his law, each one of us is a sinner, a criminal before him.

Until we understand this, the execution of Jesus Christ does not make much sense at all. But when we begin to see ourselves as God sees us, we begin to get smart. As one of the Psalms says, "The fear of the Lord is the beginning of wisdom."[10] When we begin to realize our sin and our need for God, then the execution of Jesus Christ begins to be important and we are on our way toward understanding the meaning and the purpose of this life of ours.

I am convinced that the greatest event that ever happened in the history of the world is the crucifixion of Jesus Christ. And my second reason for believing this is the crime for which he died—for your sins and for mine.

6
The Reason of It All

As we come to the threshold of this greatest event of all time, we find Jesus in the garden of Gethsemane praying.[1] Shortly after he finishes praying, a band of men—possibly as many as 200—come to capture him. They carry clubs, swords and lanterns. Of course, he has been in the temple and on the streets of Jerusalem, and they could have captured him there, but they were afraid of the people. Now they hunt him down as a common criminal.

At this point impetuous Peter draws his sword to defend his master; he swings and cuts off the ear of one of the servants of the high priest. But Jesus tells Peter to put back his sword, reminding him that those who live by the sword shall also die by it.

Then he tells Peter something extremely important. He could have said the same thing in a different way, but this is what he said: "Don't you think that I could ask my Father, and he would at once send more than twelve legions of angels to defend me?" What he is saying is this: "Look, Peter, if I wanted to get out of this I could." And it is easy to imagine how some 40,000 angels could have not only cleaned out the band of men that had come to take Jesus but could have wiped out all Caesar's legions in Palestine and laid waste the Roman Empire.

I think of other ways that Jesus might have said the same thing to Peter. He might have asked him, "How many blind men have you seen me heal? Don't you realize that I could temporarily blind these men and while they were stumbling through the trees you and I could be long gone?" Or he might have chosen to remind Peter of that day on the Sea of Galilee when the storm was about to engulf the boat. "Peter, remember how afraid you were? And remember also what I said and what happened. Don't you think that I also have the power to create storms, and that I could now cause a storm that would bring confusion so that men would only be seeking their own safety, and in the confusion you and I could easily escape?"

Whatever he could have said, the point is

clear: Jesus had not been finally overcome by his enemies. It was not that in his struggle with them they had finally won out. No, Jesus was going to his death because he was choosing to go—because he cared for you and me, in fact, because he loved us.[2]

After being captured, Jesus was brought to trial, and before he was sentenced to die on a cross, he stood in four different law courts before four different judges.[3] He stood before the Jewish Sanhedrin, probably in two phases; he stood before Herod; and he stood before Pilate at two different times. But we need to be reminded as well that he was standing before the Judge of all men, before his Father in heaven.

There are many things that are different and unique about the various trials of Jesus. One is that Jesus made no great effort to defend himself. Today it seems before charges are even placed, a man is calling for his lawyer. But Jesus did not ask for a lawyer, nor did he take up his own defense. He did answer some questions, but he made no effort at all to defend himself.

Now it wasn't that he could not make a good defense, for he could. Before the Jewish Sanhedrin he could have quoted at length the law of Moses and affirmed his commitment to this law, and not only that but he could have shown how he had kept this law perfectly. For Jesus did not come to abolish the law but to fulfill it.[4] When men from this same Sanhedrin had previously tried to trap him, he had always come out on top. To be sure, Jesus could have made a successful defense before the Jewish Sanhedrin.

Before Pilate he was charged with saying that taxes should not be paid to Rome. He could also have made a great defense against this. There had been a time when the Jewish leaders brought money to Jesus and asked whether or not it was right to pay taxes to Caesar, hoping somehow to trap him. But Jesus had said, "Whose inscription is on this coin?" And when they replied that it was Caesar's, he said, "Render to Caesar the things that are Caesar's, and to God the things that are God's."[5] Even though Jesus attempted no self-defense, Pilate concluded that he had done nothing worthy of death, for he said that he found no crime in Jesus at all.

And certainly he could have defended himself before his Father in heaven. He could have appealed, "Oh Father, you know not only my outward actions but my inner thought and my very motives, and you know that at every point I have sought to do your will, that I have fulfilled what was written in the law, 'I come to do thy will, O God.' "[6] But Jesus made no effort to defend himself here either.

It seems to me that by his silence Jesus was pleading guilty. In fact, I believe that Jesus was guilty. He was guilty because he was standing in my place and in your place and in the place of every man who would ever live.

He had never done anything wrong, but because he stood in our place and in the place of all mankind, he was guilty of lying and cheating, of murder, of hate and of every evil thought and evil action that has ever taken place. The Bible says that God caused Christ who himself knew nothing of sin actually to be sin for our sake so that we might be made good with the goodness of God. [7]

And not only did he accept the verdict, but he went out to pay the penalty. From the hall of judgment he was turned over to the men whose responsibility it was to nail him to the cross. History tells us that it was not unusual at all for the soldiers assigned to the job of the crucifixion to get about half drunk because crucifixion was a gory business, and somehow it was easier that way. And so, the eternal son of God allowed half-drunk Roman soldiers to scourge him and to crucify him. We are told on this particular day the whole battalion came out to participate in the crucifixion.

The starting point was scourging. Jesus' robe was removed and the whip came across his back, but it was more than a whip. Fastened into the end were pieces of metal and glass that dug into the flesh and tore it away as the whip was withdrawn. Sometimes in the wanton cruelty of the executioner, the whip was allowed not only to go across the back but over onto the stomach and even sometimes to the face. It is not hard to imagine that with the whole battalion watching, pressure was put on the man wielding the whip to really do a job. We do not know exactly how much he did in injuring Jesus Christ, but we do know that by the time he got to the cross it was difficult to recognize who he was.[8]

But don't get carried away with the ugliness and horror of it all. We need to be reminded again that Jesus was doing this because he loved us enough to take our place and to suffer for us in order that we might be forgiven.

After the scourging, the soldiers decided to have some sport. Since he said he was a king, they put a robe over his bloody back and decided, too, that he needed a crown; so they made one of thorns and pressed it onto his head. Every king needs a scepter, so they gave him a stick, but before they gave it to him, they beat him with it. Then they blindfolded him and took turns walking by and slapping him saying, "You are a prophet, tell us which one of us hit you." And as though they had not stooped low enough, they took turns spitting in his face. And Jesus took all of this because he deeply loved you and me.

Then they took him to the place outside the city where they crucified men, to the place called Calvary or the Skull. There they nailed his hands and feet to the cross, raised it up and dropped it in a hole prepared for it.

Most people agree that crucifixion was the

worst way ever devised to execute a man. Today, in our so-called civilized world, we hardly ever execute a person, but when we do, it is very quick—the electric chair or the gas chamber. Even the hangings of our early history were an easy way to die, but crucifixion was miserable and painful. And this was the way Jesus died.

There is a danger for us as we look at that cross to think of what he did in only a very general way, and, of course, there is a sense in which it is general because it is for all men. But it is extremely individual as well. The eternal son of God was hanging on that cross, the one who, with his Father, had cast a universe in space—a universe so big that our most powerful telescopes can't begin to see it all, and yet a universe so small that a microscope can't get to the heart of it.

A God this great and powerful and infinite is capable of knowing you and caring about you as an individual. And not only is he capable, that's the way he is through and through. He loves you. And as you look at Jesus dying on that cross, you need to forget for a minute about the fact that it was for everybody and realize that Jesus, knowing exactly what you are like, loved you enough to die there—just for you.

As he hung there, the people around the cross mocked him and hurled abuse at him: "If you are the son of God, step down from there." It struck me one day how utterly simple it would have been for Jesus Christ to step down from that cross. The one who created all that is could have easily dissolved the nails and the rope that held him to that cross.

But there is something that hit me even harder. It occurred to me what I would do if I were in his position. I wouldn't take it. I would assert who I was. I would prove to them I was God. I would come down from that cross in a blaze of glory and scare them to death. But not so with Jesus Christ. Instead he prayed, "Father, forgive them; they do not know what they are doing."[9]

If Jesus Christ had come down from the cross, we would be without hope, our sins would not be forgiven and there would be no salvation. But Jesus stayed there and died. He loved us that much. He was willing to take the mocking and all it cost to forgive us completely.

But I believe that all the pain and abuse that Jesus suffered on the cross was only a small part of what he went through to pay in full for the sins of the whole world. It was there somehow for us to see, to help us understand because we have known some pain and can understand to some degree what he was going through and therefore realize how much he must have loved us.

But all this physical suffering was at the hands of men. Because Jesus Christ had taken our place, because he had taken on our sin, he suffered also at the hands of God. And the one who did not cry out at any of the beatings that men gave him before the cross and on the cross did cry out at one point: "My God, my God, why have you forsaken me?" The only sensible explanation I have ever heard of this statement is that God had poured out his wrath on his own son and had turned his back on Jesus because Jesus was accepting the responsibility for our sins. So Jesus Christ, who in brutal physical pain said nothing, now cried out in awful suffering and loneliness as his Father punished him for our sins.

We cannot completely understand all that went on at the cross in the payment of our sins, but the words of Jesus Christ, "It is finished," are not a dying gasp but a cry of victory. It is finished—the job he came to do is done. The sin of mankind is paid for in full, and the resurrection of Jesus Christ on the third day is God's official stamp of approval that his son had accomplished the task. Later on, Peter summarized what happened: "Remember that Christ the just suffered for us the unjust, to bring us to God."[10]

My third reason for saying that the crucifixion of Jesus Christ outside Jerusalem nearly 2,000 years ago is the greatest event that ever happened is this: Jesus' death opens the way for you and me to come to God.

We who have shattered God's commandments and made ourselves totally unacceptable to him can now come to God and find forgiveness and acquittal through the penalty-paying death of Jesus Christ. We who have left God out and have gone our own way and have become his enemies can now come to God and find friendship and love through the reconciling death of Jesus Christ. We who don't make sense on our own and who desperately need to be related to God before we can find out what this life is all about can now come to him and find meaning and fulfillment. For Jesus' death is life-giving. We who have death and destruction ahead can now come to God and find eternal life because Jesus died for us that day.

No sin is too great. Christ has died for all the ungodly. Even a Charles Starkweather—with eleven murders to his negative credit—can come to God and be forgiven. And, by the way, there is evidence that he did.

The chasm between God and man, which was caused by man's sin, was bridged by the death of Jesus Christ. Paul summarizes it well: "And we can see that it was while we were powerless to help ourselves that Christ died for sinful men." In human experience it is rare for a person to give his life for another man, even a good man. Of course, a few have had the courage to do it. Yet God's love is more amazing, for it was *"while we were sinners* that Christ died for us. Moreover, if he did that for us while we were sinners, now that we are men justified by the shedding of his blood, what reason do we have to fear the wrath of God? If, while we were his enemies, Christ reconciled us to God by *dying for us,* surely now that we are reconciled we may be perfectly certain of our salvation through his *living in us.*"[11] In another place Paul writes, "Under this divine 'system' a man who has faith is now freely acquitted in the eyes of God by his generous dealing in the redemptive act of Christ Jesus. God has appointed him as the means of propitiation (payment), a propitiation accomplished by the shedding of his blood, to be received and made effective in ourselves by faith."[12]

7
The Man with the Box Seat

When something important is going on, we want to be there. The more important it is, the greater the urge. Besides that, we would like to have a good view, a good seat on the fifty yard line.

On that great day in history, on that greatest day of all, there was a man who had a front-row seat, a box seat at the greatest event in the history of the world. At first he did not appreciate it. And that really isn't surprising, for the man I am talking about was one of the criminals who was crucified with Jesus. But there he was, suspended between earth and heaven. No one could crowd in front of him; no one could obstruct his view. And although at first he had very little idea of what was going on, he was about to see firsthand the greatest event that ever happened.

I'm sure at first you would think that this man was very different from us. But it appears to me that in some ways he was quite similar to you and me, that the differences are only a matter of degree.

He seems opposite to us because he is a convicted criminal, and we are relatively decent, law-abiding citizens. True, this man was a criminal, convicted by the Romans, and certainly wrong before God's law. But we, too, are wrong before God's law. Probably he had broken it more seriously than we have, but that's only a matter of degree. All of us are sinners—all of us have broken the laws of God.

Of course, he also looks different from us because he is about to die. His life could now be measured in hours, and soon in minutes and seconds. You and I may be relatively young and healthy, but here again we need to be reminded that this is merely a difference of degree, for perhaps the most obvious fact of life is that, whether we grow old or not, all of us—rich and poor, good and bad—must die.

There is a third way that we are similar to this man. From his box seat, he had an excellent opportunity to observe the crucifixion of Jesus, but you and I have also had an excellent opportunity to observe his death. Because we live in the Western world, we have had many opportunities to hear about Jesus and what he did. And if we have been exposed to church or to some Christian movement, or if we have taken the opportunity to read the Bible or any number of books on Christianity, we have also had the chance to observe the crucifixion of Jesus.

So, since we are not so different from this man, perhaps we can learn from him something about ourselves. As we first observe him, we find him joining the crowd around him in mocking Jesus.[1] At one point the record says that he hurled abuse at him; criminal that he was, he was probably quite adept at this.

But why did this man mock Jesus? What had Jesus ever done to him? What could he possibly have against Jesus? Nothing, so far as we have reason to believe. It seems to me that the man was just doing what he had done many times before. He was doing what the crowd around him was doing and they were mocking Jesus. His attitude had no mark of individual decision—he was just following along.

And I have a sneaking hunch that many of you who read this book hold certain attitudes toward Jesus simply because of the crowd around you. If your crowd happens to be the type that would mock or make fun of Jesus, then that is what you do. Or, if your crowd happens to be one that thinks Jesus Christ a fine, good and noble man, this may be the thought you carry as well—not necessarily because you are convinced, but because the people around you seem to feel that way. Each one of us is in danger of evaluating Jesus not on the merits of his case, but on the basis of the influence of others.

Before going any further, may I remind you that it is not a good idea to form an opinion on the basis of mass approval. It's especially dangerous when the issue is significant. And what is more significant than a decision about Jesus?

I would, therefore, appeal to you. I would appeal to what is strongest and finest within you. Promise yourself, not me or anybody else but yourself, that whatever you decide about Jesus Christ you will decide on the merits of the case and not because the crowd has influenced you one way or the other.

This man with the box seat started out by mocking Jesus. But he stopped. The record does not say why he stopped, but it is obvious that he had begun to do his own thinking. I think one might go further. Perhaps he realized that his own voice was getting weaker; perhaps he looked at his own hands and saw the steady drop of blood from the wounds and realized that with every drop he was a little bit closer to death. Whatever the reason, he stopped mocking. I don't know what it takes to make a person stop thinking with his crowd and do his own thinking about Jesus Christ. Perhaps it is a different thing for different people. I do know that each person needs to reach that point.

The thief on the cross was aware that death was near. Perhaps you have heard someone say that when you are close to death your whole life flashes before you. I have never been close enough to death to verify this statement, but I would not be surprised if it were true. And I think that when the thief began to think about himself and his own life, he stopped going along with the crowd.

In all probability he was Jewish and as a child had been taught from the Old Testament. We don't know how he moved into his life of crime. Perhaps he just began running around with the wrong group, and what started out to be pranks later turned out to be crime. One thing may have led to another and it became easier to steal than to work. Possibly he and some of his cohorts had become quite professional. Maybe they robbed some of the caravans that crossed Palestine, and to get what they wanted they had to kill. And then the day came when he was captured and convicted by the Romans.

But now, as he looked back over his life, he realized that he had been a loser. It was not merely that he had been caught by the Romans, but as he looked deep into his life he recognized that he had never really found what life is all about. For a while it had seemed great getting so many things, and then he was consumed with getting more. And there were the times when looking forward to wine, women and song in Damascus he felt that he was really reaching out to life. But he had been to Damascus many times, and he knew within his heart that life was more than wine, women and song or anything that he had found.

Probably when he stood on trial before Pilate he had plead not guilty. But now he was getting honest with himself, and he turned to his fellow criminal who was still mocking Jesus and reminded him that, unlike Jesus, the two of them were getting exactly what they deserved. Jesus had never done anything wrong in his entire life.[2] But both of them were wrong before the Romans and wrong before God.

If we compare ourselves to this criminal in outward appearances, it looks like things are going pretty well for most of us. But perhaps a lot of people are like the student who told me, "Things go great as long as I'm busy, but the minute I really have to be quiet and think, I realize I don't have the answers." It's tough to be honest with ourselves. It's hard to admit that we are wrong before God and that we haven't found much to life. But it is the beginning step and this criminal had taken it. He had given up on himself.

There wasn't much use in thinking any more about his own life, so he centered his attention on Jesus, the man on the center cross. In all probability he had heard quite a bit about Jesus long before now. It is altogether possible that he had stood on the edge of a crowd one day and had listened to what Jesus had had to say. Perhaps he wasn't sure that all the things he had heard about Jesus were true, but certainly he knew that Jesus wasn't a criminal worthy of death but a good man who went around doing and saying great things.

Perhaps he was in Pilate's court standing trial when Jesus was brought in. Pilate had asked Jesus if he were a king, and Jesus had answered that his kingdom was not of this world. In fact, as Jesus put it, he had come into the world to bear witness to the true kingdom which was not of this world.[3]

Now the thief strained to look at the man on the center cross to see if Jesus could possibly be who he claimed to be. From outward appearance Jesus was merely a badly beaten man who had lost to his enemies. But there was something about him that would not let the thief give up so easily. Perhaps he began to think how he would feel if he were innocent and nevertheless had been convicted and nailed to a cross. What would he do if he were innocent and had been mocked in his dying hour? He would mock them back; he would curse them with his dying breath.

But as he looked at Jesus he saw none of this hate; he heard no curses. Instead, as he looked at Jesus he heard him say, "Father, forgive them; they do not know what they are doing."[4] Perhaps this is what tipped the scales to make him see who it really was on the cross beside him. Possibly he also recalled hearing his parents read from the old prophet Isaiah: "All we like sheep have gone astray, . . . and the Lord has laid on him the iniquity of us all."[5] Whatever he did or didn't understand about what was going on that day, he had come to his conclusion—he knew who was hanging with him. Indeed, it was the King, the Messiah, the Savior sent from God.

I suppose it would be easy for us who live so many centuries later to think that if we could only have been there, we could have seen what this man saw. And yet, this man saw beyond the battered body of Jesus. Of course, we too have to look beyond the skepticism that is so much a part of our day, but we have before us the record of the fantastic life of Jesus and the fact of his impact on our world. There is sufficient evidence for us to come to the same conclusion that this one dying there was indeed who he claimed to be—the Savior of the world.

The thief on the cross had come to believe two most important and basic doctrines of Christianity: (1) the sinfulness of man—his inability to find life on his own and his inability to keep God's law and earn his place in heaven, and (2) the fact that the man dying on that cross that day was God and Savior. Still, if the thief had died at that moment, he would not have entered Jesus' kingdom. Today as well there are many relatively decent Americans who make church to some extent a part of their life and who believe the basic teachings of the Christian faith but who, nevertheless, are in the same position as that thief.

But this criminal was getting serious. Death was too close, his own failure too obvious and the one on the center cross had become magnificent. He called out to him, "Jesus, remember me when you come into your kingdom." And by this he was saying, "I know who you are, you are the heavenly King." He was also saying, "I need you, I want you, remember me when you come into your kingdom." In reality, he was praying.

And then from the lips of Jesus came some of the greatest words ever recorded: "I tell you truly this very day you will be with me in heaven." Why could Jesus say this to that man that day? Could he say, "You'll be with me in heaven because you're a good guy"? No, in fact, it was obvious that this man was bad. Yet Jesus could say this to him because Jesus knew that he himself was paying for that man's sins and for the sins of the whole world. And to this criminal and to every man who reaches out to Jesus in faith saying, "I need you, I want you," the same answer is assured: "When you die, you'll be with me in heaven."

As the record says elsewhere, "For God so loved the world that he gave his only Son, **63** that whoever believes in him should not perish but have eternal life."[6]

Someone once said that some people are eighteen inches away from heaven. That's just the distance from the head to the heart. There is a great difference between believing facts about Jesus and believing in Jesus Christ. There is a great difference between reciting or even believing a creed and personally committing one's life to Jesus Christ. I once studied the word *believe* as John uses it in his record of Jesus' life. It appears over ninety times. One of the questions I asked myself was this: "What is the object of belief?" And time and time again the answer was Jesus Christ himself. Believe *in* Jesus Christ—believe *on* Jesus Christ.[7] And these are quite distinct from believing *about* Jesus Christ.

Here's an illustration. I have been told that there actually used to be a man who tightroped across Niagara Falls; it is said that he even carried his manager across on his shoulders one day. Let's suppose two men were watching this event and one said to the other, "Do you believe that he could carry you across on his shoulders?" And the man said, "Yes." But then the tightrope walker came over and asked the man to climb on his shoulders. The refusal came quickly. In short, there is a big difference between believing that Jesus Christ is God and Savior and climbing on his shoulders in commitment. It is one thing to believe that certain facts are true, and another thing to give our lives to him as Lord and Savior.

Jesus Christ wants to come into our lives to be our Savior and Lord and friend. He is pictured as saying, "Behold, I stand at the door and knock; if anyone hears my voice and opens the door, I will come in."[8] A painter once depicted this scene, showing Jesus standing by the door of a house. When someone pointed out to the painter that he had forgotten to put a latch on the door, he replied that he had done it on purpose. The latch is on the inside. God will never barge into our lives. He wants to come in, but he leaves the choice with us.

Step one to beginning a relationship with God is to recognize our own need—to see that we are sinful and helpless, to know that on our own we cannot really live life now or after death. It is to repent—to turn away from our sin and self-centeredness and look toward God. *Step two* is to recognize that Jesus Christ provides the way to real life. It is to understand that Jesus is God and Savior and that in his dying on the cross he paid the penalty for our sin and self-centeredness and opened the way to God. *Step three* is to personally reach out to Jesus Christ in faith, not just to believe *about* him, but to believe *in* him. Here we put our trust in him and climb on his shoulders. Here we reach out in prayer and ask him to come in and take over our lives.

And we can be certain that if we ask him in, he will come in, for he has promised, "If you open the door, I will come in."

He is ready when you are. You can put this book down right now and ask him to come into your life. There are no secret words to say, no secret ways to say them. It is a personal transaction between you and God, and when you ask him in, he comes in with a whole new relationship. A life begins that never ends.

In a new and personal way we begin to see why the crucifixion of Jesus Christ is the greatest thing that ever happened, for through Christ and what he did there that day we have come to find forgiveness and eternal life.

8
A Very Close Second

From time to time when I have spoken to people about Christ's crucifixion being the greatest of all events, someone has challenged me by saying that he thinks that the greatest event that ever took place is the resurrection of Jesus Christ. I'm pleased when I hear this, for I know that someone has been doing some good thinking. Indeed, there are only two events that can seriously challenge the crucifixion for the number one spot—Jesus' incarnation and his resurrection.

All three events depend on one another. Take away the incarnation—that God came to earth as a man—and the death of Jesus is meaningless and his resurrection is impossible. Take away the crucifixion, and men are still lost and hopeless. Without the crucifixion, the incarnation and resurrection only remind us that there is no hope. Take away the resurrection, and the incarnation and crucifixion merely play out the tragedy of God. But, together, they tell the story of good news to you, to me and to mankind.

Chapter III talked about the incarnation—about that beautiful truth that the eternal Son of God took on human flesh and lived among us. It is only fitting that now we consider Christ's resurrection.

The resurrection is meaningful to us in many ways. To begin with, it loudly confirms who Jesus Christ really is. Paul writes that Jesus "was declared Son of God by a mighty act in that he rose from the dead."[1] Also, certainly, the resurrection can be viewed as God the Father's official stamp of approval on what Jesus had done on the cross. And Jesus himself had said, "It is finished."[2] The resurrection now says, "Yes, indeed, it is finished." The job of paying for the sins of the world is completed, and men may come to God finding forgiveness and eternal life.

And, of course, to every Christian the resurrection says that we don't have to be afraid of death, for "It is sin which gives death its sting. . . . All thanks to God, then, who gives us the victory . . . through our Lord Jesus Christ!"[3] In his dying on the cross Jesus took the stinger out of death, and in his resurrection proved that he had power over death and could raise us from the dead as well. As Jesus said to Martha at the tomb of her brother Lazarus, "I myself am the resurrection and the life. The man who believes in me will live even though he dies."[4] In another place the Scripture says, "Do not be afraid. I am the first and the last, the living one. I am he who was dead, and now you see me alive for timeless ages! I hold in my hand the keys of death and the grave."[5] Jesus' resurrection proves that these are not empty words.

There are many ways that the resurrection speaks to us, but there is one more which I would like to mention. The resurrection of Jesus helps confirm the truthfulness of Christianity. There is no way that we can actually prove that Jesus rose from the dead. Believing on Jesus as Savior and Lord will always require a step of faith. But the evidence we do have for the resurrection shows that belief in Christ need not be a stupid, blind leap but rather an intelligent act of faith based on reasonable evidence.

To help us see this, we must begin by separating what is a matter of good history and what is a matter of Christian faith. To begin with, it is good history to say that a man named Jesus lived almost 2,000 years ago. We date all time by him, and men who make no pretense of believing Christian teaching nevertheless write about Jesus without ever questioning that he actually lived. On the other hand, to say that Jesus was God in the flesh is a statement of Christian faith. It is good history to say that Jesus was crucified by the Romans outside Jerusalem. But when we begin to describe what he was doing on the cross, we are talking about Christian doctrine.

When we come to the resurrection, it appears that it is also good history to say that the tomb of Jesus was empty on the third day. To say that he rose from the dead is a matter of Christian faith. The first stories spread around to discount the resurrection do, indeed, accept the fact that the tomb was empty. If this is so, how did it get that way? Down through the years the opponents of Jesus have proposed many theories to explain it.

One of the stories passed down to discount the resurrection suggests that the women went to the wrong tomb. In their sorrow and emotion and tears, they ended up at the wrong grave. I can see how this might have happened. Women are like that sometimes. They cry and lose their sense of direction. Certainly these women loved Jesus dearly. His death had been a great shock to them. But I imagine that when they ran for the disciples, Peter and John would have come back to the right tomb and would have pointed out to these emotional women their sad mistake. But even if the disciples had followed the women's leading, certainly the Pharisees and Sadducees—the avowed enemies of Jesus—would not have allowed something so simple to stand. They would have gone to the right tomb and showed to everyone the body of Jesus Christ.

The enemies of Jesus had gone to great pains to get him out of the way. They had risked their own positions with their own people, for Jesus was popular. They had risked their relationship with Pilate, the Roman governor who did not want to execute him anyway. They had gone all out to get Jesus out of the way. So, when people started to say that Jesus had risen from the dead, you can be sure that, if the women had gone to the wrong tomb, these men would have found the right one. In fact, if there were any way to produce Jesus' body they would have produced it. They would have displayed it in the temple and squelched forever the rumor that Jesus had come back from the dead. But they could not come up with the body. It wasn't there.

It is amazing that we should owe a debt to the enemies of Jesus, but we do. During his public ministry, Jesus referred many times to the fact that he would die but that he would rise again on the third day.[6] It is strange that his disciples should forget this. When he died, they were afraid and ran for fear the same thing should happen to them. But the enemies of Jesus remembered. So they went to Pilate and said, "Sir, we have remembered that while this imposter was alive, he said, 'after three days I shall rise again.' Will you give the order then to have the grave closely guarded until the third day, so that there can be no chance of his disciples' coming and stealing the body and telling people that he has risen from the dead? We should then be faced with a worse fraud than the first one."[7] In response, Pilate told them, "Go and make it as safe as you think necessary." And they went and made the grave secure, putting a seal on the stone and leaving the soldiers on guard. Imagine that—Roman soldiers guarding the dead body of Jesus.

When, on the third day, Jesus did rise from the dead, the guards were struck with terror. And well they might be. When they recovered, some of the sentries went into the city and reported to the religious leaders. The whole religious hierarchy got together, talked it over and bribed the soldiers, saying, "Your story must be that his disciples came after dark and stole him away while you were asleep. If by any chance this reaches the governor's ears, we will put it right with him and see that you do not suffer for it."[8] So that's what the soldiers did.

But let's take a closer look at their story and see if it holds up. It shouldn't take long to see that there is one ridiculous fault with it. If they were asleep, how did they know what happened? Any third-rate lawyer would

see through that one and have the case

thrown out of court.

But there are more holes in the story. It is difficult for me to imagine that Jesus' friends who were afraid and ran when he was captured would all of a sudden risk their necks breaking the seal of Rome and laying themselves open to attack by Roman soldiers just to steal a body that wouldn't do them any good.

But, for the sake of argument, let's assume that this is what happened. Let's say that the disciples hid in the area near the tomb and that they carefully watched the sentries until each one of them had fallen asleep. Then they crept to the tomb, being careful not to wake them up. Let's say also that they were able to break the seal and to move the stone and that, before any of the guards stirred, they were able to remove the body from the tomb and escape. And, then, in the dark of night, they went to a very deserted spot, dug a grave, put the body in and covered it up. And then, after a period of time, they went back to the temple and announced to the people that Jesus had risen.

I suppose for a while it might be possible to imagine that this had happened. After all, these men had not been very important people until they became associated with Jesus. But with him, they were in the public eye. They had been known and honored by many people and maybe now they figured that, by telling them that Jesus had risen from the dead, they could maintain their prominence.

One could actually believe this except for one important factor. For telling people that Jesus had risen from the dead, these men were taken before the same Sanhedrin that had sent Jesus to his crucifixion, and they were warned to say no more of it on pain of severe punishment. Nonetheless, they replied that it was more important for them to do what God said than to stay healthy by obeying the Sanhedrin.[9] In due time, they were punished—beaten, imprisoned and eventually killed.

Now, I don't know for sure about you, but I know that, if I were one of the disciples and my back was bared and bent over, I'd do some serious thinking. The first time that whip came across my back, I would clearly remember the night we dug the grave and dropped the body in it. The second time the whip came down, I'd think how foolish it was to suffer for something that I knew was a lie. With the third stripe, I'd recall that fishing was a pretty good job after all and, before they hit me again, I'd yell, "Stop! I'll tell you where the body is."

But it didn't happen that way. The disciples went away from their beatings to tell again the account of Jesus' resurrection. As we observe the disciples in the months and years that followed, one thing becomes obvious. These men had not stolen a body and reburied it in a shallow grave. Men do not suffer and die for what they know is a lie.

They were men who were absolutely convinced that Jesus had risen from the dead.

Tradition tells us that all the disciples except John met violent deaths because they persisted in telling the world about Jesus. They were willing to die for him because they were convinced that he had conquered death and had offered to them a life that was eternal. This handful of men changed the course of history. The story of the resurrection was not written by "nice little men" who sat in pleasant monastaries thinking pleasant thoughts about life after death. The story of the resurrection of Christ was written by men who were willing to write the pages of history with their own blood.

The tomb of Jesus was empty on the third day. The stories proposed by Jesus' enemies to explain how it became empty just do not fit the facts. The explanation that best fits the facts of history is that Jesus Christ did, in fact, rise from the dead. The lives of his disciples confirm to later ages the truth of the resurrection.

And, when the Roman empire began to persecute the Christian faith, it took on a difficult task—in fact, an impossible one. It was not Christianity that broke under Rome, it was the Roman Empire which bowed to Christ. In A.D. 313 Emperor Constantine issued an edict of toleration, and in A.D. 325 he made it the official religion of the Roman Empire. No one can prove that Jesus Christ rose from the dead; but we, as Christians, can hold our heads high, for the evidence concerning the resurrection makes it reasonable to put our faith and trust in him.

9
From Here to Eternity

It would not surprise me a bit if someone jumped to the conclusion that, once he understood the meaning of the crucifixion of Jesus, saw the significance of the resurrection and accepted Christ as his Savior and Lord, then the cross fades into the background. But it just is not so. The cross is rightly the symbol of Christianity and it stands at the center of the Christian faith. This can be shown in a number of ways, but some strike me as being uniquely significant.

To begin with, there is the matter of assurance. Most Christians at one time or another doubt whether they have really accepted Jesus Christ and are a part of God's family.

This doubting probably strikes the new Christian the hardest. Unfortunately, many Christians tend to base their assurance on feelings or on their performance. They look back to that time when they asked Christ into their heart and they remember the warm glow and the good feeling that accompanied their decision. And now in the routine of life, they don't feel that way any more. So they fear that they are lost again.

Other people look at the quality of their lives—their own shortcomings, failures and sins—and realize how far short they have come from acting like a Christian should act. And since their lives don't glow, they conclude that they couldn't possibly still be a Christian.

But the Christian's relationship to God is determined by neither feeling nor performance. It is true that from time to time feelings are an important part of being a Christian, but feelings come and go and are not, and should never be considered, the basis of our relationship to God. It is true, of course, that when God enters our lives, we should begin to become different. But progress is often painfully slow, and the time will never come when our performance is good enough to earn us entrance into the family of God. There will always be a gap between what we are and what we ought to be.

We are not Christians because of how we feel or how we perform, but because of what

Jesus Christ did for us on the cross. He did all that needed to be done to make it possible for us to come to God. Our big line was, "Help!" There is nothing that we can add to his sacrifice.

When you begin to doubt your relationship to God, look at the cross and realize afresh that you belong to the family of God because of what Christ did there that day.[1]

Assurance of being in God's family is closely related to the fact of forgiveness. Too many people who start the Christian life feel that when they have sinned they have blown it all. Perhaps they were always afraid that they couldn't make it, and now they have just proven their point. But when Jesus died, he knew what we were like. He knew what we had done before we trusted him, and he knew what we would do afterward. So he was dying for all our sins.

The Christian life is not over when a person fails any more than a child's life is over when he trips taking his first steps. God doesn't give up on us. He is anxious to help us get up and start again.

Forgiveness is built into the cross. Some new Christians seem to be quite aware of this at first, for they have sinned and found forgiveness. But when they have to come back again and again to ask forgiveness for the same sins and failures, they get uptight. The Bible gives no warrant for this. It puts no limit on the number of times we can obtain forgiveness. It simply says, "If we confess our failures, God is faithful and just to forgive us for them, and he washes us clean from all our wrong-headedness."[2] God is actually being faithful and just on the basis of what his son did on the cross.

One might think this is too easy. I can sin, find forgiveness, sin again and always find forgiveness—hence a sort of freedom to sin. But I have not found it so. When I come back again and again to the Savior to seek forgiveness, I find instead a whole new sense of gratitude for what he did for me, a whole new appreciation for what he accomplished on my behalf. And I also go away with a new motivation to live right for him. When you sin, don't wait, come quickly to the cross and find the forgiveness that Jesus purchased for us there.

In the cross we see love in a way we see it nowhere else. Everyone needs love. People who understand the human race best realize how much every individual needs love. Perhaps the worst experience in the whole world is to feel that nobody really cares for us—nobody really loves us. A Christian can always be assured that someone loves him. Even when all earthly friends and relatives seem to turn away, there is the constant assurance of God's love. The cross is its greatest demonstration.[3] In those times of loneliness, don't wait, remember that God loved you enough to suffer and die for you.

The cross really helps us to understand the

Christian life. Too many people believe that, when they trust Jesus and seek to follow him, all their daily hang-ups will disappear. And then when things don't go right, they become frustrated. Somehow they come to believe that this Christian life isn't any good after all. But the Christian life is difficult, and that's not surprising. For when we set out to follow God in a world that isn't following him, it is obvious that we are heading upstream, swimming against the current.

Looking at the cross gives us a better understanding of this struggle. For here even Jesus Christ, the one who followed his father perfectly, found himself in the midst of deep conflicts. In fact, his enemies tried to do away with him by nailing him to a cross. We need to understand that doing the Father's business in a sinful world is tough.[4]

Along with this understanding we can find courage. When things get tough, when it seems that we are being pushed around by forces both within and without, when we have the desire to give up and follow the path of least resistance, then we need to look again at the cross for courage. Here we find the one who never did a single thing wrong taking his undeserved punishment like a man. He was whipped and mistreated, but he did not cry out. He was mocked and abused, but he prayed for the forgiveness of his opponents. And in the overwhelming struggle he took time to heal the ear of one of his opponents and to answer the request of a crook.

So when things get tough, don't wait, look at the cross, look at the man there, take heart, find courage and press on.

As we look at the world around us we see people suffering—suffering because of poverty, discrimination, handicaps, illness—the list is endless. Our first inclination is to close our eyes or turn away. We always seem to have enough problems of our own. But when we look at the cross, we see one who left comfort to enter a world of suffering. We see one who cared enough to die even for those who hated him. So when you look at a world in need and find your heart cold, don't wait, draw near to the cross and let Jesus' compassion warm your heart and move you to reach out in love and concern to those who need you.

In the cross there is purpose. In this crazy, mixed-up world, so many people do not know where they are going. In a day that has experienced utterly fantastic technical progress, we have lost contact with meaning and purpose. All around us, men speak of a purposeless universe and a purposeless life.

But Christians can look to the cross and find purpose. We begin by seeing our own value, a value demonstrated by the fact that God loved us enough to die for us. Then we realize that at the head of this universe is a God who loved and cared enough to enter our world and to bring salvation. And so we find purpose here.

We learn to live for Jesus and to tell the rest of the world the good news about him. As Paul says, "The love of Christ compels me, for we are convinced that if one died for all, then all have died, and therefore those who live should not live for themselves but for the one who loved them and gave himself for them."[5] That is, the whole purpose of our life is tied up with God. We were made for him in the first place and now through Jesus we can live according to God's desire and to our own great joy and fulfillment. Part of that joy comes in telling a dying world the good news of Jesus—that there is forgiveness, that there is salvation, that there is life eternal.

In our life time we will follow a number of minor purposes. We will seek to win the game, to make the team, to win the championship, to be elected or accepted in a particular group, office or college. Throughout life there will be short-term purposes that are important and have their rightful place.

But here is a purpose that never ends. It has meaning and value in every situation. What a great God we have: He has given you and me the opportunity to share in his work by telling the rest of the world about his love.[6] So when meaning and purpose seem vague, don't wait, come back to the cross. See the purpose of the Savior, reach out to the people around you and point them to the cross.

And this new life that Jesus Christ gives us never ends. We need to be constantly reminded of its eternal aspect. We need to know that on the cross Jesus Christ purchased heaven for us. When we put our trust in him we immediately find salvation from the *penalty* of sin and we begin to find salvation from the *power* of sin. But a very real part of the salvation that Jesus provided is the eventual salvation from the very *presence* of sin.

Someday we will experience the freedom from sin, from pain and suffering, from hate and cruelty, and from everything that messes up the life we know now.[7] So when the wretchedness of the world around tends to overpower you, don't wait, go to the cross for hope and comfort, knowing that there Jesus Christ made it possible for us to enter into his eternal heaven.

I am confident that when we get to heaven we will have a whole new appreciation for what Jesus did on the cross. But even now, from here to eternity, the cross is of prime importance. For there we find assurance, forgiveness and love, understanding, courage and compassion, meaning, purpose and the bright hope of eternal life with our Savior and our Lord.

10
The Sky is not the Limit

When we enter into fellowship with God, we enter a relationship that has no limits. God is infinite and eternal, and there is no danger that a human being will ever exhaust the possibilities of this new life with God. Even the greatest of Christians would confess that in their lifetime they have only begun to scratch the surface of the wonder and beauty of knowing God.

At the same time they confess that they have found what they are looking for. As Paul wrote, "Yes, and I look upon everything as loss compared with the overwhelming gain of knowing Christ Jesus my Lord."[1]

It has been rightly said that man has a God-shaped vacuum that only God can fill.

Along the way in our experience with God we come to plateaus and we suffer defeats, and at times it is difficult to see the completeness of the life that we have with our God and Savior. But I would testify that, even in the dark moments and certainly in the bright ones, in my life with Jesus Christ I have found fulfillment.

The Scriptures bear witness to the fact that whatever we have experienced of God in this life is merely a beginning. John writes, "Here and now we *are* God's children. We don't know what we shall become in the future. We only know that, if reality were to break through, we should reflect his likeness, for we should see him as he really is!"[2] Later he writes, speaking of heaven, "See! The home of God is with men, and he will live among them. They shall be his people, and God himself shall be with them, and will wipe away every tear from their eyes. Death shall be no more, and never again shall there be sorrow or crying or pain. For all those former things are past and gone."[3]

As a high school friend of mine said, "One of the great things about Christianity is that it doesn't peak out." His statement rang a responsive chord deep within my own life.

When Jesus Christ died on that cross outside the city of Jerusalem nearly 2,000 years ago, he made it possible for us to be forgiven and to enter into this relationship with God that never ends.

There's no doubt about it—the death of Jesus Christ on the cross for our sins is just the greatest!

INDEX OF SCRIPTURE REFERENCES

chapter III—WHO WAS HE?
   [1] Mark 4:1, 35-41.
   [2] John 6:68-69 (RSV).
   [3] John 1:1-4, 14.
   [4] John 10:30 (RSV).
   [5] John 8:58 (RSV).
   [6] John 9:35-39.
   [7] Acts 14:8-18.
   [8] Mark 14:61-64 (RSV).

chapter IV—TIME OUT FOR A WEDDING
   [1] John 2:1-11.
   [2] 1 John 1:1-18; 1 John 1:1-4.

chapter V—THE CRIME OF IT ALL

1 John 18:38 (Phillips).
2 Matthew 27:3-5.
3 1 Peter 2:22.
4 1 Corinthians 15:3-4 (RSV).
5 1 John 2:1-2
6 Exodus 20:1-17.
7 Colossians 3:20.
8 Romans 13:11-14 (Phillips).
9 Romans 3:10-23 (Phillips).
10 Psalm 111:10 (RSV).

chapter VI—THE REASON OF IT ALL

1 Matthew 26:36-56; Mark 14:32-52; Luke 22:39-53; John 18:1-13.
2 John 3:16.
3 Matthew 26:57—27:26; Mark 14:53—15:16; Luke 22:54—23:25; John 18:12—19:16.
4 Matthew 5:17-18.
5 Mark 12:17 (RSV).
6 Hebrews 10:7.
7 2 Corinthians 5:21.
8 Isaiah 52:14.
9 Luke 23:34 (Phillips).
10 1 Peter 3:18 (Phillips).
11 Romans 5:6-10 (Phillips).
12 Romans 3:24-25 (Phillips).

chapter VII—THE MAN WITH THE BOX SEAT

1 Matthew 27:38-44.
2 Luke 23:40-43.
3 John 18:33-37.
4 Luke 23:34 (Phillips).
5 Isaiah 53:6 (RSV).
6 John 3:16 (RSV).
7 John 1:12, 50; 2:11, 24; 3:16, 18, 36; 6:28-29, etc.

8 Revelation 3:20 (RSV).

chapter VIII—A VERY CLOSE SECOND

[1] Romans 1:4 (NEB).
[2] John 19:30.
[3] 1 Corinthians 15:56-57 (Phillips).
[4] John 11:25 (Phillips).
[5] Revelation 1:17-18 (Phillips).
[6] Matthew 16:21; 17:9, 22-23; 20:18-19.
[7] Matthew 27:63-66 (Phillips).
[8] Matthew 28:13-14 (Phillips).
[9] Acts 4:1-22.

chapter IX—FROM HERE TO ETERNITY

[1] Romans 3:20-28.
[2] 1 John 1:9 (paraphrase mine).
[3] 1 John 4:9-10.
[4] John 15:18-21.
[5] 2 Corinthians 5:14-15 (paraphrase mine).
[6] 2 Corinthians 5:20.
[7] Revelation 21:3-4; 22:3-5.

chapter X—THE SKY IS NOT THE LIMIT

[1] Philippians 3:8 (Phillips).
[2] 1 John 3:2 (Phillips).
[3] Revelation 21:3-4 (Phillips).